o.P. 1966

OUCH!

1966 CATALOGUE

18⁰⁰

Clyfford Still

Thirty-three Paintings in the

ALBRIGHT-KNOX ART GALLERY

The Buffalo Fine Arts Academy
Buffalo, New York
1966

Published by The Buffalo Fine Arts Academy

Buffalo, New York, 1966

All rights reserved

Library of Congress Card Number 66-15942

Printed in England by Percy Lund, Humphries & Co. Ltd

Color engravings by Gilchrist Brothers Ltd, England

Photographs by Creative Color Inc., New York City

CONTENTS

---

*. . . After seeing many of
Clyfford Still's works I have
come to the conclusion that
he is a sorcerer with powerful
magic. . . . Nay! An Earth Shaker*
CLAY SPOHN – 1947

11. 1947–8–W No.2

108½ × 88 inches

THE publication of this catalogue records the appreciation of The Buffalo Fine Arts Academy of the magnificent gift it received in April 1964 of a selected group of paintings by the distinguished artist, Clyfford Still. Ranging in years from 1937 to 1963, they represent the development of his work which has been so influential on the art of our time. Added to the two important acquisitions of the red and black painting *1954* and *1957 D No.1*, the collection of Clyfford Stills in the Albright-Knox Art Gallery now consists of thirty-three paintings.

Each of these is reproduced in color in this catalogue.

The Buffalo Fine Arts Academy is deeply grateful to Mr. Still for his generous gift and for the opportunity it has given the Albright-Knox Art Gallery to display this superb collection to the public for study and enjoyment now and in the years ahead.

SEYMOUR H. KNOX, *President*
The Buffalo Fine Arts Academy

8

THE collection of the Albright-Knox Art Gallery is heavily concentrated on works of art dating from the early 1940's when the focus of the contemporary art world moved from Europe to the United States.

Shortly after World War II, Clyfford Still emerged as the leader of that sudden, vital – and unprecedented in this country – upsurging of exceptional creative energy and productivity. His work and his influence in this particular American revolution have been of the utmost importance in art history since that time.

While other artists are represented in our collection by one, two, or three works, these 33 paintings, executed over 26 years, afford an opportunity to study this painter's work in both breadth and depth. A single painting by Clyfford Still is an experience; a broad survey of his work is a revelation of the full impact of his images and the immense power of his statements. We consider it a unique privilege to own and exhibit these paintings.

I would like to take this opportunity to express my personal appreciation to Clyfford Still not only for his generous gift which has so significantly enhanced the collection, but also for his cordial and friendly relationship with both the Gallery and myself. He has been unfailingly cooperative over the years of our association. Most recently, he has worked closely with us in the preparation of this book.

In that connection I would like to thank Mrs. Clyfford Still, Mrs. Katharine Kuh, and Miss Ethel Moore for their invaluable contributions to the text and to the production of this record of the unique collection of Still paintings at the Albright-Knox Art Gallery.

GORDON M. SMITH, *Director*
Albright-Knox Art Gallery

FOREWORD

EACH year sees certain artists of our century intrenched more solidly as indispensable leaders. From America I think immediately of Clyfford Still. Yet when I try to put my thoughts into words I stumble, for the language of art turns hollow these days from over-use. And since Still deals with intangibles and imponderables, any evaluation of his paintings becomes doubly tenuous. His canvases, like living organisms, permit no one element to exist alone. No color, no brush stroke, no void, no surface detail is separate from the whole. All are interrelated precisely as the forces of nature are interdependent.

To visit Still's studio in Maryland and see his chronological progression is to recognize uncompromising growth. Individual canvases appear less important than the continuous flow of his work. It is not single pictures, no matter how impressive, that convey the artist's thinking; it is the uninterrupted sequence of painting after painting that reveals his cosmos, a cosmos inseparable from our own world of fluid movement and weighted tensions.

No one better than Still understands the boundaryless dimensions of modern space. Before "space" became an esthetic stereotype, he was probing its meaning as relentlessly as scientists were investigating its physical properties. Turning space into yawning, shredded voids, he early explored the immaterial world that lies beyond our immediate sights, and in so doing broke ground for an entire generation of artists.

At the beginning it was the living figure that engrossed his attention, but in later years the figure became fused with limitless space. Throughout, it is fusion that plays a basic role in all Still's paintings. "I never wanted color to be color. I never wanted texture to be texture, or images to become shapes. I wanted them all to fuse into a living spirit," he said recently. Again, in discussing an extraordinary group of black paintings done around 1948–49 (a group, by the way, that even now

10

is not without marked influence in America) Still observed, "Black was never a color of death or terror for me. I think of it as warm – and generative. But color is what you choose to make it."

The man is his work. The two cannot be separated. I doubt if anything could have sidetracked Clyfford Still. And one feels the same about his paintings. Majestic, serious, sometimes somber, sometimes exhilarating, they seem to grow of their own free will. Nothing contains them, nothing stops them. How exactly they were painted seems irrelevant; it is their total impact that counts. These canvases are not built on themes about life; they are an extension of life, a key to ourselves, to our pierced universe, and, above all, a key to Clyfford Still. For him, "Art is the only aristocracy left where a man takes full responsibility. To turn art into a carnival stunt is," he says, "a contemptible exercise".

Still left New York four years ago to settle in the lovely rolling country of Maryland. Here, in comparative isolation, his work has noticeably changed. The recent paintings, vast in scale and totally liberated from any fixed focus, sweep upward with frank exuberance. Measured and disciplined as always, these surging open canvases bear witness to a new optimism, to an escalating power.

KATHARINE KUH

Photograph by Sandra Still

BIOGRAPHICAL NOTES

I wanted a life I could respect. As a man, it became necessary for me to repudiate the degenerating luxury of "conformism" and accept the responsibilities of clarifying and extending the living forces inherent in the disciplines of freedom.

CLYFFORD STILL

Letter, August 25, 1965

Clyfford Still was born November 30, 1904, in Grandin, North Dakota, where his parents, of Scotch and Irish ancestry, had emigrated from Canada. Shortly after his birth, the family moved to Spokane, Washington. His father worked there as an accountant, but in 1910 he homesteaded in southern Alberta, Canada, near Bow Island and for the next ten years they moved back and forth almost every year.

During his youth, he drew and painted at every opportunity, training himself in perspective, light, texture, and color. He was also deeply interested in music and the hours he had free were spent either painting, studying reproductions, the history and theories of art, or at the piano. When he was 20 he made his first trip to New York, arriving at the Metropolitan Museum of Art before the doors opened. He was, however, disappointed in what he saw. He found something missing, some statement that he felt profoundly and did not find in the work of the European masters. Having decided that he should pursue a more formal art education, he enrolled in a class at the Art Students' League but found that disappointing also, and left after 45 minutes. The exercises and results he observed he had already explored for himself some years before and had rejected most of them as a waste of time or as destructive. He spent a few weeks touring the galleries and museums of the city, studying the past and present painters' work at first-hand. Disillusioned, he shortened his stay in New York and returned west.

Still completed his last two years of high school at Spokane University Preparatory School. He enrolled at Spokane University where he was given a scholarship in art. He graduated in 1933 and that fall went to Washington State University

13

in Pullman as a Teaching Fellow. He received his M.A. degree in 1935, and remained on the faculty as an Instructor (1935–40) and an Assistant Professor (1940–41).

Although Clyfford Still has been a highly influential teacher, he chose that career only because it allowed more time and energy for his painting than any other. His faculty friends were rarely other art teachers, but members of the music, English, philosophy, and mathematics departments, reflecting the wide variety of his interests.

During the summers of 1934 and 1935 he was a Fellow at The Trask Foundation (now Yaddo) in Saratoga Springs, New York. These months were the first in many years when he was completely free from both farm work and teaching and mark an important period in his life. He did a series of figure studies in oil, some of them painted on old green windowshades because he could not afford canvas. He describes these paintings as bordering on the Tragic but they mark the beginning of his moving away from painting as reacting to that which one experiences from outside, to his concept of painting as an instrument of comprehension.

The next five years were spent in "painting through" the contemporary influences and movements – the Bauhaus, Dada, Surrealism, Cubism, and the then-current Paris school. This rejection of the European tradition, beginning at the Metropolitan Museum in 1924, has resulted in the particularly liberating character of Still's work.*

When viewed chronologically, an interesting aspect of Still's work is the occasional recapitulation in a painting or a group of paintings which would seem to date from an earlier period. These represent a conscious effort which he made whenever he felt the work in danger of becoming repetitious, facile, or too influenced by material. Then he found it necessary to review an earlier approach and reaffirm his purpose.

From fall of 1941 until summer of 1943 Still worked in the war industries – aircraft and shipbuilding in Oakland, California, and later in San Francisco. During these months, except for brief intervals, he put aside his art and devoted himself fully to the war effort. Only an occasional exercise in nostalgia or a portrait study as a gift for a friend were executed during after-hours to keep his discipline of hand and eye. This explains the limited number of works produced during this

* Pollock, deKooning, Gorky, Rothko, Guston, Hartigan – all these painters have some obvious link with "the European Tradition," if not with the specifically Cubist/Classical one. Everybody with any sense managed to *see* them. But Clyfford Still, who didn't bother to furnish a "statement" (the catalogue quoted some remarks from long ago) or even a photograph of himself – Still was another matter. People came up to his vast pictures very quietly, and toppled over into them without a murmur and came out with nothing to say. It was all very still. It was really wonderful to re-live the first years of his reception in California, where now, alas, the Still style has become a mass-produced cliche.   KENNETH REXROTH
                                                                          ART NEWS, Summer 1959

period. However, several exceptional and highly influential paintings were made and were included in his first one-man exhibition, a retrospective, in the San Francisco Museum of Art where he was invited to show in March, 1943.

That fall, after his completion of aircraft contracts in San Francisco, he returned to teaching and painting, this time at the Richmond Professional Institute, then a Division of the College of William and Mary, in Richmond, Virginia. Again his release from the pressures of enervating routines resulted in an explosion of energy which brought forth an extraordinary number of works and inventions in a great variety of media. He remained there until moving to New York in the summer of 1945.

Almost immediately, he was offered an exhibition at Peggy Guggenheim's Art of This Century gallery, scheduled for the following February. Both the artist and his work were well-received in New York, but once again he found the atmosphere constricting, and he returned to Canada for the summer.

That fall, 1946, he began teaching at the California School of Fine Arts in San Francisco. In the summer of 1948 he resigned from the school and went to New York to bring together a number of active artists in a teaching group to aid younger men in the milieu of New York City. He returned to the California School of Fine Arts in the fall, where he taught until 1950. There he initiated and directed the advanced painting group by which the school became especially known throughout the world.

During this time his work and ideas were becoming increasingly well known and his influence international in scope. He was invited to exhibit at the Betty Parsons Gallery, New York, in April, 1947; April, 1950; and January–February, 1951; the California Palace of the Legion of Honor, San Francisco, in July, 1947; and Metart Gallery, San Francisco (founded by a group of his students) June–July, 1950.

In 1950, Still once again moved to New York where he remained – except for occasional trips to San Francisco – for eleven years, living at 48 Cooper Square and, later, at 128 West 23rd Street. He exhibited in the *15 Americans* show at the Museum of Modern Art, New York, April–July, 1952. He had a major one-man exhibition of 72 paintings at the Albright Art Gallery in November–December, 1959, and exhibited 32 paintings in a one-man show initiating the Institute of Contemporary Art, University of Pennsylvania, Philadelphia, October–December, 1963.

Some of Clyfford Still's published statements are to be found in the catalogue of the *15 Americans* exhibition at the Museum of Modern Art, 1952; in the catalogue for his one-man exhibition at the Albright Art Gallery, 1959; in *ART NEWS*, Vol. 62, No. 7, November, 1963; and in *ARTFORUM*, Vol. 11, No. 6, December, 1963.

Since 1961, he has worked and lived in seclusion near Westminster, Maryland.

ETHEL MOORE

A STATEMENT BY THE ARTIST

To supplement the reproductions of paintings shown in this catalogue with written comment by the painter represents not only the extreme of temerity on my part – it is patently presumptuous. At least that is what I have been told by some of those who write about pictures. In a culture where the written word is commonly regarded as synonymous with God, the gesture suggests an arrogance pregnant with blasphemy. Having been instructed in the degrees of my apostasy I am left no choice but to confirm their long repeated convictions – add weight to their thesauri of my crimes.

By the end of my twenty-fifth year, having seen and studied deeply the works and acts of those men of art presented in museums and books as masters, I was brought to the conclusion that very few of them merited the admiration they received and those few most often achieved true worth after they had defied their means and mores. The galleries held almost exclusively a collection of works selected to reflect the quality of minds dedicated to aesthetic puerilities and cultural pretensions. And few writers revealed in their analyses or criticisms more than a very obvious desire to be authorities in the social milieu, and were as completely ignorant of the whole of painting which they befouled and presumed to direct as they were inept in the art of writing.

To me it became an imperative that if this instrument – this extension of one's mind and heart and hand – were to be given its potential, a fresh start must be made. My conclusion was born of knowledge of the past, but my understanding of the past and its influence, right up to the present moment, made it clear that it could not be escaped by will alone. The manifestos and gestures of the Cubists, the Fauves, the Dadaists, Surrealists, Futurists or Expressionists were only evidence that the Black Mass was but a pathetic homage to that which it often presumed to mock. And the Bauhaus herded them briskly into a cool, universal Buchenwald. All the devices were at hand, and all the devices had failed to emancipate.

I had not overlooked the organic lesson; ontogeny suggested that the way through the maze of sterility required recapitulation of my phylogenic inheritance. Neither verbalizings nor aesthetic accretions would suffice. I had to accomplish my purpose, my emancipation and the exalting responsibility which I trusted would follow, totally and directly through my own life and hands. Time would have to wait. Years of labor would be required, but each work would bring its quanta of release and add the strength needed to realize the step which must ensue.

Through the years of the 1950's the work of clarifying, excising, extending and reviewing was pressed during all the time and with all the energy I could order. Until those symbols of obeisance to – or illustration of – vested social structures, from antiquity through Cubism and Surrealism to my then immediate contemporaries, were impaled and their sycophancy exposed on the blade of my identity.

Of course, trouble began when my paintings were first publicly seen. The professionals complained that they were without precedent; or that they gave evidence of traditional things misunderstood. Aesthetic, political, even religious offense was apparent! To make assault plausible crypto-Christian moralities were applied to me in terms brashly devised to misinterpret every facet of my life and meaning. Judgment was given and published.

The compliment was returned. Because now I had proof that my years of painting and deliberation had not been wasted. Only, the work had to be carried on in aloneness and with ruthless purpose. I had learned as a youth the price one pays for a father, a master, a Yahweh, or his contemporary substitute – an Institutional Culture. But my crime was compounded. To sin against the Order in the lighted arena was no deep offense; one could be dealt with – analyzed, neutralized, or encysted. But for one to defy the laws of Control, in the silence of the catacombs, with the canon instrument of their aggrandizement – for this more than correction was needed – this was treason!

Here was I free and here was I betrayed by my failure to withdraw completely from those who know me. Surely that which they found of interest should be shared with others. That the "others" responded with resentment or fear only stimulated their desire to justify their interest. Always in terms that would convince. Rational, artistically adequate, socially acceptable terms. Reminding my defenders that their efforts bore the germs of negation of all that gave these canvases meaning and purpose for me, I was made aware that the professionals *had* caught the odor of a latent power, smelled qualities that could be exploited.

For these conceptions could be perverted into pretentious exercises in design, parodied as socio-aesthetic devotions, or mauled into psychotic alibis expedient for ambition or intellectual impotence. The elements of my paintings, ineluctably co-ordinated, confirmed for me the liberation of the spirit. In the hands of unscrupulous and calculating men it was readily apparent that these elements could be segregated and evacuated to intimidate the mind, blast the eyes with hatred, or seduce with insipid deceit.

Meanwhile, literary frustrates, and political aficionados posing as painters, leapt forth to affirm their dedication to Progress, People, Peace, Purity, Love, or the *avant-garde*. Examples purporting to be my antecedents were hauled out and indiscriminately compared with my work. Fatuous generalizations obscured every particular. Thus the genesis of a liberating absolute was buried under a blanket of historical inanities.

I have been told, to my considerable amusement, that my personal departure from New York City was hailed by many remaining there as "a victory for their Establishment." Certainly, acquiescent replacements from coast to coast – ex-students and perennial imitators alike – were happily hustled forth to deny that I had ever existed. So was authority restored to the institution of Art; and the crafting of histories resumed by those who would starve should their hoax be exposed. A Pyrrhic charade.

Let it be clearly understood that my relation to that contemporary Moloch, the Culture State, has not been altered. In its smothering omnipresence there is no *place*, ideologically or practically, for anyone who assumes the aspiration by which birth was given to the paintings reproduced in this catalogue. Few institutions that would survive among the power structures of our culture can afford the presence of an individual who would challenge the merit of their rules, nor dare they embrace a code of conduct or administration that does not seek, and yield to, the collectivist denominators of this time.

Mr. Seymour Knox and Mr. Gordon Smith, two men who in my eyes have shown exceptional independence from the role their duties demand of them, invited me to place a group of my paintings under the care and protection of the Albright-Knox Art Gallery. Upon hearing my qualifying terms, their agreement was immediate. My concern that the pictures be kept together required that they be held permanently and continuously in the Albright-Knox Art Gallery – not permitted to be shipped from the museum to any other gallery or city. Yet for those who are unable for any reason to travel to the museum, or who would have a pictorial index of that part of my work which is in its care, a book of reproductions would be made. The present volume of thirty-three color plates, which includes two large works purchased several years ago by the Gallery, is their complement to my bequest.

Thus, paradoxically, a fragment of a means to freedom, thrust with resolution and commitment through the cultural boundaries of this era will, I trust, be made visible for those who desire to see it in the terms in which it was originally conceived.

I must add that the onlooker should bear in mind that the prodigal son has not returned to the father. But, rather, in passing and holding his pride as a mandate of his honor, he brings a gift no man will regard with contempt if he respects his own soul.

To all who would know the meaning and the responsibilities of freedom, intrinsic and absolute, these works are dedicated.

Clyfford Still

CLYFFORD STILL

1. **1937–8–A**
    $47 \times 33\frac{1}{2}$ inches

2. 1941-2-C
    $42\frac{1}{2} \times 32$ inches

3. 1945–K

50 × 31 inches

4. July 1945–R
69 × 32 inches

5.   September 1946
     $60 \times 27\frac{1}{2}$ inches

6. 1946–L

71 × 46 inches

7. 1946–N

71 × 45 inches

8. **January 1947**
   62 × 45 inches

9.   1947–G

62½ × 39 inches

10.   1947–8–A

45 × 40 inches

For Plate 11 see Frontispiece

12. 1948–B

$77\frac{1}{2} \times 69\frac{1}{2}$ inches

13. **January 1948**
  79 × 60 inches

14.   1948–E
82 × 69 inches

15. July 1948

58½ × 49 inches

16. 1948–M

58×55 inches

17.   1949
$47\frac{1}{2} \times 38\frac{1}{2}$ inches

18.   1949–C
86 × 69 inches

19. 1949–H

80 × 69 inches

20. 1949–M

$93 \times 69\frac{1}{2}$ inches

21.   January 1950–D
    94 × 69 inches

22. October 1950
  80 × 68½ inches

23. **November 1950**
    80 × 68 inches

24. November 1950 No.2
$92\frac{1}{2} \times 79\frac{1}{2}$ inches

25. 1951–L No.2
114 × 96 inches

26. 1951–E

117 × 145 inches

27. **November 1953**
     $114 \times 81\frac{1}{2}$ inches

28. 1954

113½×156 inches

29.   November 1954
114 × 95 inches

30.   September 1955
     114 × 95 inches

31. 1957–D No.1
115 × 159 inches

32. **April 1962**
115 × 158 inches

33. 1963–A

$114 \times 75\frac{1}{2}$ inches

NOTES ON THE PLATES

Height precedes width in dimensions

PLATE 1. 1937–8–A. 47 × 33½ inches.
Oil on canvas. Painted in Pullman, Washington.
Shown privately, Washington State University, 1938.
Shown privately, New York City, 1945.
Exhibited in one-man show initiating the Institute of Contemporary Art, University of Pennsylvania, Philadelphia, 1963.

PLATE 2. 1941–2–C. 42½ × 32 inches.
Oil on canvas. Painted in Oakland, California.
Submitted to one-man retrospective show, San Francisco Museum of Art, 1943.
Theme modified in wood carving made while teaching at Richmond Professional Institute, Richmond, Virginia, 1943.
Exhibited in one-man show initiating the Institute of Contemporary Art, University of Pennsylvania, Philadelphia, 1963.

PLATE 3. 1945–K. 50 × 31 inches.
Oil on canvas. Painted Cornelia Street, New York City.
Shown privately to artists in New York, 1945.
Exhibited in one-man show initiating the Institute of Contemporary Art, University of Pennsylvania, Philadelphia, 1963.

PLATE 4. July 1945–R. 69 × 32 inches.
Oil on canvas. Painted in Richmond, Virginia.
Shown privately, Richmond, Virginia, 1945.
Shown privately, New York City, Fall, 1945.
Exhibited in one-man show, Art of This Century gallery, New York City, February–March, 1946.
Exhibited in one-man show, Albright Art Gallery, Buffalo, New York, 1959.

PLATE 5. September 1946. 60 × 27½ inches.
Oil on canvas. Painted in San Francisco.
Shown privately, California Street, San Francisco, Fall, 1946.
Exhibited in one-man show, Betty Parsons Gallery, New York City, April, 1947.

PLATE 6. 1946–L. 71 × 46 inches.
Oil on canvas. Painted in San Francisco.
Exhibited in one-man show, California Palace of the Legion of Honor, San Francisco, 1947.
Exhibited in one-man show, Albright Art Gallery, Buffalo, New York, 1959.

PLATE 7. 1946–N. 71 × 45 inches.
Oil on canvas. Painted in San Francisco.
Exhibited in one-man show, Betty Parsons Gallery, New York City, April, 1947.
Exhibited in one-man show, California Palace of the Legion of Honor, San Francisco, July, 1947.
Exhibited in one-man show, Albright Art Gallery, Buffalo, New York, 1959.

PLATE 8. January 1947. 62 × 45 inches.
Oil on canvas. Painted in San Francisco.
Exhibited in one-man show, California Palace of the Legion of Honor, San Francisco, July, 1947.

PLATE 9. 1947–G. 62½ × 39 inches.
Oil on canvas. Painted in San Francisco.
Exhibited in California School of Fine Arts, San Francisco, 1947.
Exhibited in one-man show, Albright Art Gallery, Buffalo, New York, 1959.

PLATE 10. 1947–8–A. 45 × 40 inches.
Oil on canvas. Painted in San Francisco.
Shown privately, California School of Fine Arts, San Francisco, 1948.

Exhibited in one-man show, Metart Gallery, San Francisco, June–July, 1950.

Exhibited in one-man show initiating the Institute of Contemporary Art, University of Pennsylvania, Philadelphia, 1963.

Plate 11. (Frontispiece) 1947–8–W No.2. 108½ × 88 inches.
Oil on canvas. Painted in San Francisco.
(No.1 shown privately in San Francisco, 1948 and 1949, and in New York City, 1949–56.)
Exhibited in one-man show, Albright Art Gallery, Buffalo, New York, 1959.

PLATE 12. 1948–B. 77½ × 69½ inches.
Oil on canvas. Painted in San Francisco.
Shown privately, California School of Fine Arts, San Francisco, 1948.
Exhibited in San Francisco Museum of Art, at Symposium, Summer, 1950.
Exhibited in one-man show, Albright Art Gallery, Buffalo, New York, 1959.

PLATE 13. January 1948. 79 × 60 inches.
Oil on canvas. Painted in San Francisco.
Shown privately, Berkeley, California, Fall, 1948.

PLATE 14. 1948–E. 82 × 69 inches.
Oil on canvas. Painted in San Francisco.
Exhibited in one-man show, Metart Gallery, San Francisco, June-July, 1950.
Exhibited in one-man show, Albright Art Gallery, Buffalo, New York, 1959.

PLATE 15. July 1948. 58½ × 49 inches.
Oil on Canvas. Painted in New York City.
Shown privately, Cornelia Street, New York City, 1948.

PLATE 16. 1948–M. 58 × 55 inches.
Oil on canvas. Painted in San Francisco.
Shown privately, San Francisco, Fall, 1948.
Exhibited in one-man show, Betty Parsons Gallery, New York City, January-February, 1951.
Exhibited in one-man show, Albright Art Gallery, Buffalo, New York, 1959.

PLATE 17. 1949. 47½ × 38½ inches.
Oil on canvas. Painted in San Francisco.
Shown privately, San Francisco, Summer, 1949.
Shown privately, Sidney Janis Gallery, New York City, 1953–54.

PLATE 18. 1949–C. 86 × 69 inches.
Oil on canvas. Painted in San Francisco.
Exhibited in one-man show, Metart Gallery, San Francisco, June-July, 1950.
Exhibited in one-man show, Albright Art Gallery, Buffalo, New York, 1959.

PLATE 19. 1949–H. 80 × 69 inches.
Oil on canvas. Painted in San Francisco.
Shown privately, California School of Fine Arts, San Francisco, 1949.
Shown privately, 87th Street, New York City, Fall, 1950.
Exhibited in one-man show, Albright Art Gallery, Buffalo, New York, 1959.

PLATE 20. 1949–M. 93 × 69½ inches.
Oil on canvas. Painted in San Francisco.
Exhibited in one-man show, Betty Parsons Gallery, New York City, January-February 1951.
Exhibited in one-man show, Albright Art Gallery, Buffalo, New York, 1959.

PLATE 21. January 1950–D. 94 × 69 inches.
Oil on canvas. Painted in San Francisco.
Exhibited in one-man show, Metart Gallery, San Francisco, June-July, 1950.
Exhibited in one-man show, Albright Art Gallery, Buffalo, New York, 1959.

PLATE 22. October 1950. 80 × 68½ inches.
Oil on canvas. Painted 87th Street, New York City.
Shown privately, 87th Street and 48 Cooper Square, New York City, 1950–52.
Shown privately, Sidney Janis Gallery, New York City, 1953–54.

PLATE 23. November 1950. 80 × 68 inches.
Oil on canvas. Painted 48 Cooper Square, New York City.
Shown privately, 48 Cooper Square, New York City.

PLATE 24. November 1950 No.2. 92½ × 79½ inches.
Oil on canvas. Painted 48 Cooper Square, New York City.
Shown privately 48 Cooper Square, New York City, Fall, 1950.

PLATE 25. 1951–L No.2. 114 × 96 inches.
Oil on canvas. Painted in New York City.
(No.1 exhibited Sidney Janis Gallery, New York City, January, 1954; destroyed.)
Exhibited in one-man show, Albright Art Gallery, Buffalo, New York, 1959.
Exhibited in one-man show initiating the Institute of Contemporary Art, University of Pennsylvania, Philadelphia, 1963.

PLATE 26. 1951–E. 117 × 143 inches.
Oil on canvas. Painted in New York City.
Shown privately, 48 Cooper Square, New York City, February, 1951.
Exhibited in one-man show, Albright Art Gallery, Buffalo, New York, 1959.
Exhibited in one-man show initiating the Institute of Contemporary Art, University of Pennsylvania, Philadelphia, 1963.

PLATE 27. November 1953. 114 × 81½ inches.
Oil on canvas. Painted 48 Cooper Square, New York City.
Shown privately, 48 Cooper Square, New York City, 1953.
Shown privately, 128 W. 23rd Street, New York City, 1955.

PLATE 28. 1954. 113½ × 156 inches.
Oil on canvas. Painted in New York City.
Purchased by Albright Art Gallery, Buffalo, New York, 1957.
Exhibited in *Documenta II*, Kassel, Germany, July–October, 1959.

PLATE 29. November 1954. 114 × 95 inches.
Oil on canvas. Painted 131 W. 23rd Street, New York City.
Shown privately, 128 W. 23rd Street, New York City, 1955.

PLATE 30. September 1955. 114 × 95 inches.
Oil on canvas. Painted 128 W. 23rd Street, New York City.
Shown privately, 128 W. 23rd Street, New York City, October, 1955.

PLATE 31. 1957–D No.1. 113 × 159 inches
Oil on canvas. Painted in New York City.
Exhibited in one-man show, Albright Art Gallery, Buffalo, New York, 1959.
Purchased by Albright Art Gallery, 1959.
Exhibited in The Solomon R. Guggenheim Museum, New York City, 1960–61.

PLATE 32. April 1962 113 × 158 inches.
Oil on canvas. Painted in Westminster, Maryland.
Shown privately, Westminster, Maryland, 1962.
First publicly exhibited in Albright-Knox Art Gallery, Buffalo, New York, January, 1963.

PLATE 33. 1963–A. 114 × 75½ inches.
Oil on canvas. Painted in Westminster, Maryland.
Exhibited in one-man show, initiating the Institute of Contemporary Art, University of Pennsylvania, Philadelphia, 1963.